Authors' Note

Welcome to our Spriggles family! Spriggles combines "spirit" and "giggles" to motivate young children to lead healthy, active, and enthusiastic lifestyles.

It is important to recognize that while being colorful, playful, and fun, "Spriggles Motivational Books for Children" are, above all else, interactive and educational tools. These are books to be read together by parents and children, grandparents and children, educators and children, and anyone else with a sincere concern for the emotional and physical direction of our kids. As interactive tools, these books enable us to reinforce the positive messages contained on every page. When we read "Get out and about, Trout," it's an ideal time to explain to a child the importance of investigating the world around us and experiencing all the magic it has to offer. As well, when we read "Go for a jog, Frog," it's an ideal time to explain the necessity of regular exercise, and then reinforce it with "Ride your bike, Pike," and "Play in the park, Shark."

As educational tools, these books will increase a child's vocabulary with words such as "healthy," "creative," and "nature," while developing and enhancing their recognition of many different animals. We understand that a few of the words may be above the level of the younger children, but the illustrations and rhymes are sure to delight them. As these children age and their intellect develops, the stories and messages that accompany the illustrations will have a lasting effect as long as they are taught and reinforced. Please feel free to contact us at (888) 875-5856 or visit our website at www.spriggles.com if you desire further assistance with any of the concepts presented in these books.

And remember, we as parents, grandparents, educators, and anyone else reading these stories are never beyond needing a little motivation ourselves. So go ahead and sneak a peek when you need a reminder to "Get out of the house, Mouse," or "Hike a trail, Quail."

Better yet, have the kids remind you!

Freddie Frog loves to run outdoors but sometimes needs a little push to get him going.

So what do we tell fast Freddie?

"Take a jog, Frog"

Carly Caribou and her friends have fun racing down the river.

So what do we tell Carly?

"Paddle that canoe, Caribou"

Charlie Chimpanzee wants to find something fun to do outside in the winter.

So what do we tell chilly Charlie?

"Learn to ski, Chimpanzee"

Angie Antelope loves to play in the snow.

So what do we tell Angie?

"Sled down the slope, Antelope"

Amy Ape wants to have lots of energy.

So what do we
tell awesome Amy?

"Stay in shape, Ape"

Buster Bobwhite is looking for something to do on a windy day.

So what do we tell Buster?

"Fly a kite, Bobwhite"

Wally Whale would like to try
a new water sport.

So what do we
tell wild Wally?

"Set sail, Whale"

Al Albatross likes to play catch with his friends.

So what do we tell Al?

"Give the ball a toss, Albatross"

David Dolphin knows that in order to play better he needs to practice.

So what do we tell David?

"Let's go golfin', Dolphin"

Shelly Shark loves to play with her friends,
but knows it's not safe to play in the street.

So what do we
tell Shelly?

"Play in the park, Shark"

Marvin Mule knows that swimming is fun
and good for his muscles.

So what do we
tell Marvin?

"Swim laps in the pool, Mule"

Teddy Turtle loves to run and jump
but sometimes things get in his way.

So what do we
tell steady Teddy?

"Clear the hurdle, Turtle"

Gerard St. Bernard wants to play outside
but needs to stay close to home.

So what do we
tell Gerard?

"Play in the yard, St. Bernard"

Henry Hawk likes to spend time with his family after dinner.

So what do we tell Henry?

"Go for a walk, Hawk"

Trent Trout wants to learn more about
the world around him.

So what do we
tell Trent?

"Get out and about, Trout"

Brooke Bumblebee is looking for
something to do at the picnic.

So what do we
tell Brooke?

"Throw a frisbee, Bumblebee"

Sammy Snake gets bored just laying in the sun.

So what do we tell Sammy?

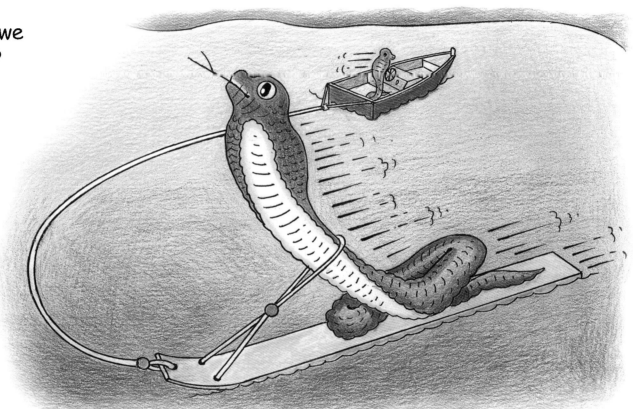

"Water-ski on the lake, Snake"

Margaret Mole is looking for something
to do on a rainy day.

So what do we
tell Margaret?

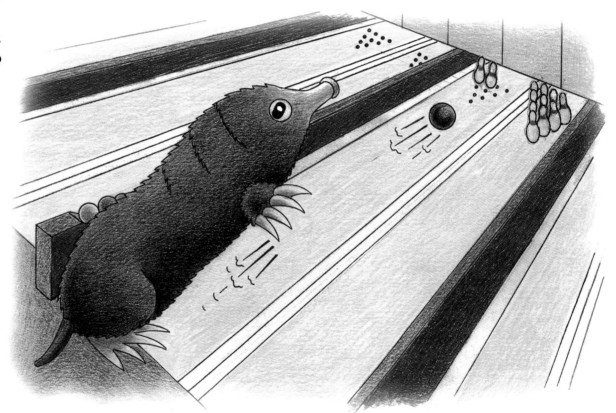

"It's fun to bowl, Mole"

Godfrey Goat needs to get his family
to the other side of the lake.

So what do we
tell Godfrey?

"Row a boat, Goat"

Paula Pike wants to visit her friends before it gets dark.

So what do we tell Paula?

"Ride your bike, Pike"

William Weasel wants to be creative.

So what do we
tell William?

"Paint on an easel, Weasel"

Bryce Blue Jay spends too
much time watching TV.

So what do we tell Bryce?

"Go play, Blue Jay"

Faith Fawn wants to help with the family chores.

So what do we tell Faith?

"Rake the lawn, Fawn"

Mindy Mink wants to do something fun for her birthday.

So what do we tell Mindy?

"Skate in the rink, Mink"

Heather Hippo loves to cool off
on a hot summer day.

So what do we
tell Heather?

"Go for a dip-o, Hippo"

Quincy Quail loves nature and wants to get some fresh air.

So what do we tell Quincy?

"Hike a trail, Quail"

Maisy Mouse gets tired sitting around the house all day.

So what do we tell lazy Maisy?

"Get out of the house, Mouse"